T0199019

Poetry

FROM THE HEART

by Poppy

E A HANVEY

WestBow Press books may be ordered through booksellers or by contacting:

WestBow Press
A Division of Thomas Nelson & Zondervan
1663 Liberty Drive
Bloomington, IN 47403
www.westbowpress.com
844-714-3454

ISBN: 978-1-6642-0647-2 (sc)
ISBN: 978-1-6642-0648-9 (e)

Library of Congress Control Number: 2020918603

Print information available on the last page.

WestBow Press rev. date: 10/1/2020

WESTBOW
PRESS®
A DIVISION OF THOMAS NELSON
& ZONDERVAN

Introduction

Poppy was a quiet, unpublished poet and this book is about his poetry.

Poppy was a romantic, home grown poet from the foothills of South Carolina. He walked the trail in the picture above many times and wrote his poems about nature, family, and home.

One of his greatest enjoyments was walking the forests and creeks on the family farm. He panned for gold and left several ounces in a small bottle, when he passed away in 1996 at the age of 72, after an afternoon of walking the farm with one of his grandsons, Alex.

His poems are unique and from the heart reflecting his strong love of his country and its freedoms.

His oldest son, Steve has compiled his poems and written one of the poems to emphasize the love of God's creatures by his father, as well as Poppy's humor. Poppy often joked with the worn old line, "you're a poet and don't even know it!"

Table of Contents

Please Hold

A kind request in tender tone
From one so lost or so alone
A supplication for one to comply
A child's anguish in a world so high.

Too high with ambition to achieve
Too selfish to listen or believe
That children need a bosom close
To cling assured in calm repose

To rich, to poor, to parents all
Awake and walk strong and tall
Material things can a wee heart break
As she cries for love, what a mistake

This world's treasure is not in gold
But in men and women with heart and soul
With minds open to a little child's plea
"Please hold" or "Come play with me".

E A Hanvey 1974

Snow In The Morning

www.bigfoto.com

A vision of white, a lovely sight,
Early this morn, I tho't it moonlight.
It silently, softly blankets the Earth
As adorning the trees, it smiles in mirth.

For such a brief time it purifys,
Hides mans' work where no beauty lies.
In that sea of white, nature blooms –
Pollution is hidden, no tho't of doom.

God's promise to man, as in the rainbow,
Is renewed on earth in the guiltless snow.
Making all beautiful, as is His plan,
Being slightly stayed by the works of Man.

Man and Nature must be in tune,
As the Indians knew, these many moons.
The snow is eternal, a light, a glow.
It will always stay, but Man must go!

E A Hanvey
2-6-83

www.bigfoto.com

The Rose

Why did God create the Rose?
Was it very carefully planned?
Did He know that friend and foe
Would share its beauty across the land?

Did He desire in its creation
Something of His love to show
To Mankind of every nation
Who live so fast – their pace to slow.

Was it to give a peek at Heaven
To us mortals here on Earth
Perhaps to add a bit of leaven
That we may rise to our own true worth.

What ere His Plan, God only knows,
But in each life, we understand
We must take time to smell the rose
And meditate, the fate of "Man".

E A Hanvey
2-5-84

God Bless Mother

Love and appreciation from a Mother's son
To all the Mothers in the world
They've struggled, strived, battled and won
A harbor of peace for boys and girls.

The Hope of generations yet to come
The precious peace of children all
The word that draws them nearer home
Where troubles arise and dreams may fall.

The foundation of the World surely must rest
Upon a Mother's sweet loving breast
She asks for little but gives her all
Standing always ready to answer the call.

The call of a child in the dark with fear
With arms outstretched she wipes a tear
The little one soon drifts off to sleep
Mother near, her quiet vigil to keep.

Such is the Power of a Mother's love
Like a beacon at night, it towers above
To surround the Earth in loving care
Her sons and daughters knowing she's there.

They rise to ambitious heights sublime
Knowing "Bedrock" will last the sands of time
With this firm footing only Mother can give
Our world will survive, Our Nation will live.

E A Hanvey
5-12-85

The Homestead

The old House upon the hill
Still sturdy, strong and memory filled.
It creaks with age and needs repair,
My childhood home – my heart is there!

The cedar logs with knots exposed
Form four columns, where clings the rose.
The porch upstairs with fancy lattice,
Summer sleeping where the breeze is at us.

Two chimneys loom large and high
Embrace and Warm the house between.
Fireplaces glow and love is nigh,
Both melt the ice; this winter scene.

At night we climbed the stair to bed,
Leaving warmth behind, cold and dark ahead.
Then comes the morn, we scamper down,
To the roaring fire but watch your gown!

All dressed now, to the morning chores;
I'll milk mine and you milk yours.
Feed the hogs and oats for the mules,
Hurry now – Almost time for school.

E A Hanvey date unknown

Class of 1941

Reunion-Revival

1986

Class of '41 is center stage
In our prime, regardless of age,
After 45, we're still the rage
Ready to turn another page.

Children have grown and gone away
Freedom again on life's highway.
And for the dreams of yesterday
A second chance to hope, to pray.

No time to sit, to ponder the past,
Come alive! Just 45, revive the cast,
Curtain up, Act III, We're here to last,
Life is great and <u>Fair</u> is the Forecast.

Renew sweet memories but keep alive
The spark that's burned these 45,
Make new memories, don't just survive,
Get "busy as a bee", build a new hive!

Retirement is for the very old,
Happy are the brave and bold
Who reach, who seek and find new goals,
<u>Never</u> quite content with <u>status quo's</u>.

E A Hanvey Spring 1986

Some of my best Friends happen to be Dogs

My dog is always glad to see me,
Even just to go outside to pee.
She never shows emotion except for glee,
A ball will turn everything positive, you see.

When it's time to rest after a long day,
My dog is always ready to go out and play.
She wags her tail and jumps for joy,
She barks and bounces at first sight of her toy.

Her fur coat so shiny and warm,
Her inquisitive look such a charm,
Her bark that almost says out loud,
"I'm ready to entertain this whole family crowd"!

Would many "best' friends want to say,
"You haven't paid attention to me today".
But how many dogs would simply sit,
As if ignoring them didn't hurt a bit.

My dog's love is without limits,
She always forgets in a few minutes,
My last impatient actions, emotional fits,
She smiles and simply sits.

Stephan A Hanvey 2009

Epilogue

The concepts of love, faith, family, home, dogs, nature, and country are
fundamental to the heart driven motives for living a full and happy life.

Poppy was a romantic at heart and an engineer by
education. He made much of his work fun for himself and
those around him by seeing many things through the eyes of a child, an innocent,
a need for caring and special feelings that come only from the heart.

These poems are visions as seen by a person with those virtues.
In a humorous vein Poppy had a dog, and named
him "Lucky Dog", not because he had found a home one evening with
Poppy, when the rest of the world had left him behind, but perhaps,
because Poppy felt like he was the "lucky" one, not his dog.

Stephan A Hanvey 2009

Notes

Printed in the United States
By Bookmasters